Things We've Thought of Enough

David Morin

Illustrated by Maki Naro

www.scholar.harvard.edu/david-morin
www.makinaro.myportfolio.com

ISBN: 978-1-7342596-0-5

Library of Congress Control Number: 2019919718

Printed in the United States of America

First Printing 2019
Cambridge, MA

Cover design by Nicola Black Design, LLC
www.nicolablack.com

Things We've Thought of Enough

You spend your life within the seats,
  staring at the stage.
You let your fears run through the years
  and never turn the page.
But if you dream of taking bows
  before a crowd that roars,
Get up, engage, and join the stage,
  and make the show be yours.

"You shouldn't make faces – they'll stick that way."
A little white lie that some grownups may say.
But watch how you act because one thing is true:
Though faces don't stick, personalities do.

We press on ahead in perpetual youth,
   with delusions we somehow mature.
The children grow older, the offspring get bolder,
   and we lengthen the crawl on the floor.
But ever we flinch and return to our crib,
   carving notches with each passing year.
In this coming of age, we turn in our cage,
   all alone on a tiny blue sphere.

From yelling "surprise," to lifting up rocks,
From rock-paper-scissors, to synchronized clocks,
It's a question profound, and I just want to know:
When do you start – on "3" or on "go"?

It really seems doubtful, so how can it be?
I'll believe only when I am able to see.
Or in view of the way that we often perceive,
I'll be able to see only when I believe.

Shipwrecked but ready, they made a new life
 and planted the seeds of the pines.
The children would sing as the trees added rings,
 and sometimes they dreamt of designs.
As decades receded, the question was when
 the grandkids would make the decree
To harvest the trees, and enter the seas
 in the boat that would set them all free.

From back in your youth, your friends of all kinds
Recall you from memories stuck in their minds –
Some of them pretty and some of them rotten,
But most of them things that you've long since forgotten.

It's rarely enough to have one time existed,
Or pushed for what's proper and two times insisted.
It's great to have stood up and three times resisted,
But real heroes come from the ones who persisted.

We stressed over this, we obsessed over that,
  there were so many troubles in sight.
We struggled and fought to conquer the thoughts
  that kept us awake in the night.
But the years bring us peace as we grow to accept –
  it's fine if life's edges are rough.
So we raise up our mugs, and sweep 'neath the rugs
  the things that we've thought of enough.

At five years old, she stomped the ground
And asked, "Why can't I turn around?"
"Just do like this…," we played a mime.
She said, "No, no, I mean in time."

Grams used to sit in the breeze of her porch
   in the shade of that giant oak tree,
With Pop and Aunt Claire playing games by her chair
   and Uncle Joe perched on her knee.
But the porches are empty, and now we just sit
   in our flickering, stacked-up blue tombs.
When a sign of the wise is the bluish glazed eyes,
   we know we're just running on fumes.

The help won't be lasting. It won't make a dent.
There are things more important. I'm already spent.
There's never a shortage of things you can say
To justify joining the turning away.

(Apologies to Pink Floyd)

If disagreements drag along,
Try your best to prove you're wrong.
If you can't, you're either right,
Or your best is rather light.

It's easy to think, from the old black and whites,
   the world had no color back then.
Gray seemed in style, with rarely a smile
   as the curtain man counted to ten.
But wait a few years, and your grandkids will say,
   as the progress progresses again,
"The colors are grand, but I don't understand
   why the world had no movement back then."

Follow the path that has only left prints,
And hop on your right so you offer no hints
For those who will follow, who then have no clue
That two are ahead – each with one shoe.

Dead Sea Scrolls and Mayan scripts,
Pompeii's rooms and pharaohs' crypts.
Across the years, each era waves
With words and bones in books and graves.

When logic is shunned beware that all claims
Enjoy equal footing, diluted the same.
There's no need for warfare and no need for spies;
For every one truth, there are millions of lies.

That single small step for a man, it turns out,
   was shorter than everyone thinks.
"We all make mistakes," he said, hitting the brakes,
   with a mortified look and some blinks.
Then taking a leap for mankind, he confirmed
   even legends themselves aren't immune.
The ship he commanded had tragically landed
   on top of the Man on the Moon.

A child once asked us what world she would find.
What would we leave her, and would it be kind?
We gave our reply with a rose in clenched fists –
Ask not if it's kind, but if it exists.

When a roadside is littered with pillars of salt,
   you shouldn't look back on what's done.
It's clear that the price for the souls who think twice
   is to melt 'neath the rain and the sun.
And even the wary can fall for the traps,
   as you see now the key to the code –
It isn't the fault of the pillars of salt,
   it's the mirrors all lining the road.

She finally came to understand
Why spirals get so out of hand.
It often seems each turn is mild,
But have enough, and things get wild.

With toes at the edge of our future's abyss,
   and heels at the cliff of our past,
Aligned side by side, a few billion wide,
   we hope that our footing will last.
Ever so slowly the ledge in front grows,
   as it crumbles from under our heels.
So we shuffle ahead, on present's thin thread,
   and dream about wide open fields.

When the curtain has dropped and the lights have gone out,
    and the cast is packed up in a box,
With their joints made of wood and the notion they could
    escape, were it not for the locks,
When the plan is the same, each day after day,
    with paupers at mercy of kings,
The semblance of will breeds the movements so still,
    as the puppets try pulling their strings.

Picture a world filled with desolate lands,
Where birds build their nests upon petrified hands,
And feet send cut roots, to pay for the crime,
As we mimic the trees in a penitent mime.

When making decisions, don't take things too fast,
You need to examine both future and past.
Don't dwell on the now. Don't stare at your feet.
But *do* look both ways like you're crossing a street.

Your voice is so soft, I'm unable to hear.
My eyesight has faded, so please draw in near.
But the trouble is more than the senses I seek,
You hear me so faint, I'm unable to speak.

You'll let those things slide, some evils are fine –
    the justified price of a cause.
You'll turn a blind eye, and sometimes you'll lie,
    as you brush aside all of those flaws.
But soon you'll be sliding and grasping a thread
    of what you had thought was a rope.
You look like a tool with that ends-and-means drool
    that greases your slippery slope.

Some say fire. Some say ice.
Some say either would nicely suffice.
But maybe it's neither, and simply the plan
That we ask how it ends, when it never began.

(Apologies to Robert Frost)

I follow your path through the blistering sands,
Where vision turns white and we grope with scorched hands.
But high from above, through the heat, one can see
A ring in the sand; perhaps you follow me.

How can you tell you're no longer a kid?
You stop your bike gently, no need for a skid.
In hide-and-go-seek games, you want to be found,
And puddles are things that you now walk around.

It's not always bad if we reap what we sow.
In lessons we learn, and in learning we grow.
The real problem comes from the patterns we keep
And the circles that form when we sow what we reap.

One for the hopscotch we played in the rain,
Two for the marbles that roll down the drain.
Three for the chalk lines that bend in the years,
Four for the children who follow the spheres.

Five for the swing sets that taught us to fly,
Six for the feeling we never would die.
Seven for lifetimes we cannot foresee,
Eight for the branches we add to the tree.

Nine for the vessel, this home we call earth,
Ten for the memory lost in our birth.
Eleven for sailing a sea with no end,
Twelve for the chimes to begin once again.

Letters and pictures and sympathy notes
  and pieces of distant old friends
Follow your life through the joy and the strife
  in a little box worn on the ends.
Years down the line, you'll remove from a shelf
  the memories long overdue,
And wonder once more, whose shoeboxes store
  old pictures and pieces of you.

Winter to spring, summer to fall,
   we turn through our seasons of four.
We march to the beats and perform the repeats,
   it seems like we've been through this door.
But sometimes we turn, at just the right time,
   and catch with a glimpse in our eyes
The ghosts and the fairies and wide-eyed canaries,
   whenever they drop their disguise.

It's common to lash out when losing the game
And spend your time looking for someone to blame.
Just don't be the fool in a plan so cliché
And get duped by the culprit and look the wrong way.

Reflecting long back on her earlier days,
She saw she had changed, in so many ways.
It's always a shock when on careful inspection
You see someone else in your present reflection.

What was it you said, as we sat on the swing,
  on that evening in '73?
With room for two, and nothing to do,
  we counted the stars we could see.
I asked should we care if we missed one or two,
  and you answered just like a true friend.
You whispered a no, for stars come and go,
  but moments like this never end.

"Practice makes perfect," we hear all the time,
    but sadly it just isn't true.
A form that's erratic or flaws systematic
    will limit the things you can do.
Your body will move how you train it to act,
    and not how you think that it should.
It takes practice that's perfect to make you be perfect,
    instead of just pretty darn good.

We dine through the ages with those we hold dear.
   At the table, we each play our role.
The younger ones grow, and the older ones go,
   and the stories gain ever more soul.
When the music winds down and it comes time to leave,
   the elders pass on what was theirs.
So we sit at our tables and add to the fables,
   all along playing musical chairs.

When falsehoods keep on pouring down
And facts are left to slowly drown,
We'll never see and never hear
The truths before they disappear.

The children were born to Mom and to Pop.
   They lived and they learned and they grew.
But more things are learned than the ones they discerned,
   they knew only half what they knew.
They did what they saw and they felt what they sensed,
   nothing was left for the dice.
Mom liked to mutter, and Pop used to stutter,
   so the kids grew up softly and twice.

We've long since outgrown all the endings of old.
  The final one comes from within.
There's no need for wars, or reapers at doors,
  who pale as we beckon them in.
We sail on through time to mysterious lands,
  weaving maps on our destiny's loom.
With a toast and a cheer and a dime to the seer,
  we head to our special new doom.

The bully's harm, you long endure.
The racist thinks you're not as pure.
The sexist says be more demure.
All because they're insecure.

Ever since youth, he couldn't quite add.
   Even "2 plus 2" mocked him with 3.
Try as he might, he could not get it right,
   but someday he knew that he'd see.
And finally one day, it became crystal clear –
   it wasn't a matter of smarts.
In these greatest of times, we've all lost our minds
   to a whole so much less than its parts.

The millennia passed as the creatures remained
  trapped on the walls of the cave.
Were they drawn to keep score, for religious decor,
  or reminders on why to be brave?
Or maybe some lad came to realize there's more
  to life than just seeking to eat.
And thus he did start this pursuit we call art,
  with a "Hey, guys, this really looks neat!"

His fear he'd mess up and be wrong made him stall.
He played it too safe and did nothing at all.
Mission accomplished, but not very bright,
For likewise he never did anything right.

History's generals act out their lines,
　bequeathing a dwindling list.
Napoleon shivers since Caesar crossed rivers
　with a die clenched so tight in his fist.
They're all simply captives of previous acts,
　brief threads on a lengthening strand.
So the history books gained their whittled new look
　when the die flew from Caesar's tied hand.

He dreamt he could fly and soar high on his wings
   away from this dead-end old town.
He'd break from the mold and the forces that hold
   the dreamers so close to the ground.
But they clipped off his wings, and weighted his boots,
   and beckoned him back from the door.
With no plan for escape, he hung pieces of tape,
   catching flies as he evened the score.

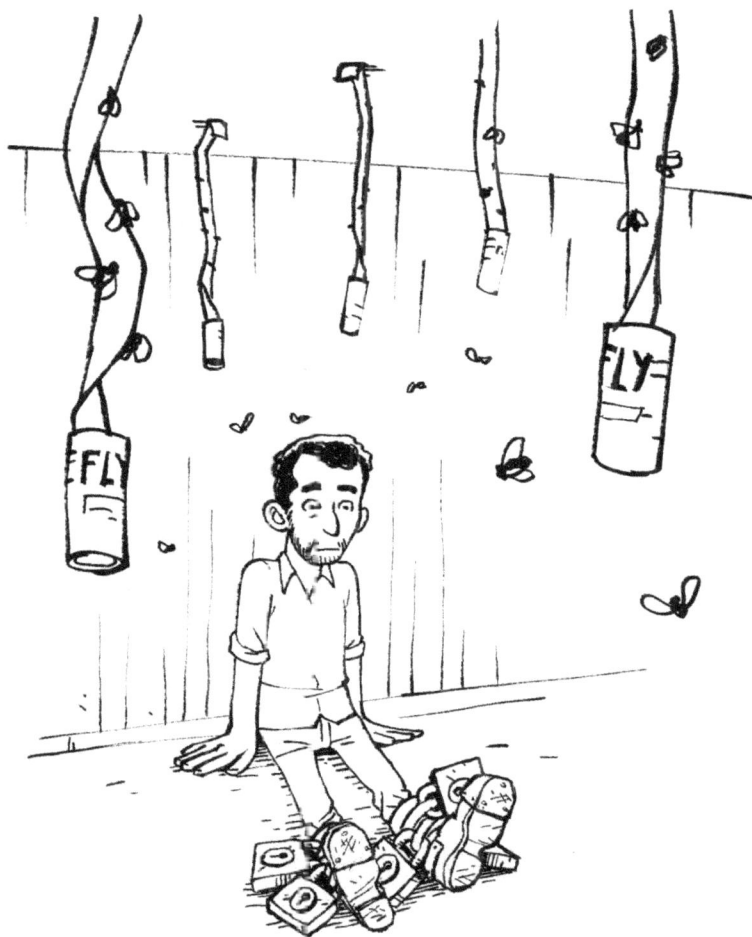

Attack me again with your sticks and your stones,
And, yes, you just *may* end up breaking my bones.
But name-calling earns you the hapless disgrace
Of failing to logically argue your case.

The truth, she would say, depends on the time,
    the future can never be wrong.
Then she whispered the tune, "I love you," but soon
    the past laid its claim to that song.
Somewhere between, we discover what's real,
    as the present looks back on its youth,
When our sweet-flowing words were divided in thirds,
    with one for each part of the truth.

That cute little toddler who can't count to two
Will grow up and someday know much more than you.
Generations will always push back the frontiers,
In slow-motion leapfrog played down through the years.

Why did that person just give me that look?
  Did I say or do something so wrong?
Perhaps it was *this*? Or did *that* cause the diss?
  Good heavens, the list is so long.
But before one proceeds to get tied up in knots,
  there might not be such a morass.
In explaining their face, it could well be the case
  they're really just bloated with gas.

All the things we said we'd do
    that never came to pass
Slip away as days and years
    recede a bit too fast.
But time is not what truly curbs
    the goals that we pursue.
Instead it's all the things we did
    we said we'd never do.

Our stories at bedtime bestowed on us keys
    to wonders and magical doors.
We lived what was read as we dreamt in our beds
    and built castles on living room floors.
But the magic erodes and the mystery fades
    until everyone seems like a pawn.
So we lie in our beds and now wonder instead
    where the kings and the queens have all gone.

The ocean of knowledge, humanity's gift –
   we all want to add to its store.
We sit in the sand and develop a plan,
   throwing pebbles each day from the shore.
When the years have grown thin, and we run out of stones,
   and the tide recedes out to the rim,
We take off our socks and then pick up some rocks
   and head down to the sea for a swim.

They grew together, they grew apart,
Alone again, just like the start.
Each of them, when all was done,
Was less than two, but more than one.

It … he thought, but he couldn't quite think,
   the newborns are always too young.
It had … he knew, all the while he grew,
   been right on the tip of his tongue.
It had always … it seemed, as he looked up the line
   at photos from color to gray,
It had always been … as it would be again,
   it had always been … that way.

Intelligent people are never so smart
  when their logic is trumped by their views.
The wisdom that's seen is the difference between
  one's bias and formal IQ.
No matter how brilliant a person may be,
  take note of the net-effect rule:
With preconceived notions and unchecked emotions,
  a genius becomes but a fool.

Sometimes we know we should try something new,
    but it's scary to take that new road.
It's safe in the past, and the future's so vast,
    it's hard to get into that mode.
We start with an amble as cars pass on by,
    and then look for a ride for a bit.
We stick out our thumbs but still lay down the crumbs,
    hoping someday we'll fully commit.

It's not so hard to comprehend
That if we cause the world to end,
We then won't have the luxury
To say, "No, wait – best two of three!"

When giggling kids at nursery school
  can melt you with their looks,
I want to know why *do* some grow
  from dears to jerks or crooks.
The wise surmise and analyze
  and endlessly discuss –
What's the force that wrecks their course?
  Surprise! It must be us.

Baggage unchecked has a penchant to spread
And affect other things that reside in your head.
Though time often makes the effects disappear,
The effects of effects are the things you should fear.

At quarter past nine on the Fourth of July,
   we bolted on home in the night.
Back in our yard, we knew how to guard
   that willow-tree image of light.
Does life mimic art, or does art mimic life?
   We were too young for thoughts so sublime.
So we laid out our pillows and gazed at the willows –
   our fireworks frozen in time.

See me once, see me twice,
Paths do cross when trailing mice.
But see me thrice, and then once more,
And never will we find the door.

Your reasoning often is molded to fit
    whatever you want to conclude.
Cherry-picked facts and circular tracks
    are signs that your logic is skewed.
You twist and you turn as you spiral on down,
    lost in the depths of delusion,
Where deep in the hollows your reasoning follows
    in retrograde from your conclusion.

He shuffled along, hunched on his cane,
   over trails that he'd run on so fast.
He was older than then, but younger than when
   today would be part of the past.
Right in between, it's a relative world,
   and we choose from the two ways to see.
So at age ninety-four, he limped all the more,
   saying, "Youth won't be wasted on me."

There are so many memories stored in our past
That will never be thought of, despite how they last.
Recalling a thought is like throwing a dart;
To remember the memories – that's the hard part.

It's always the plan when the going gets rough,
The weak have a tactic that makes them feel tough.
They look for the bait and find something to click on,
And queue up a new group of people to pick on.

The sculptor begins with one cut of the stone.
The painter's first stroke hovers all on its own.
It's tougher than peering through dense fog or mist,
An artist can see things that don't yet exist.

Rock me once more in the old wooden chair,
And lament for our elders who could not be here
To gaze on the wonders each day brings anew,
Which will all be forgotten when chairs beckon you.

Why is it hard, when you find out you're wrong,
    to admit it and not sit and stew?
Even just to yourself; set aside on a shelf
    what anyone thinks about you.
Perhaps it's because, if there now is a case
    where your viewpoint was shown to the door,
With no end in sight, when you think you are right,
    you can never again be so sure.

The excuses we make for not reaching a goal,
The conjured-up forces beyond our control.
We decry the injustice and seethe at the crime,
Shackled with straw and boxed in like a mime.

Each athlete lives the glory days,
   atop the highest ground.
But every peak and record streak
   is sure to come unwound.
So seize the day, but have a plan
   for life without the ball.
For in your prime, the sands of time
   begin their steady fall.

He always has trouble in making decisions;
   forks in the road make him freeze.
For every decision, his brain sees revisions;
   vending machines are a tease.
Perhaps he could choose by just flipping a coin?
   Even *that* question makes his head pound.
And whenever his car enters roundabout tar,
   he endlessly circles around.

Never at all, in his wildest dreams,
  did General Stanley Bernard
Believe that his days would conclude in a haze
  of shots from the firing squad.
And he never imagined that someday he'd know
  his foe like the back of his hand.
In his blindfolded poise he detected the noise
  and smell of his childhood land.

Believing the end of repeated abuse,
Trusting a liar with one more excuse.
There's nothing to fix and no need for a cure,
Since things will be different – this time for sure.

A rustle so faint, from deep in a well –
   acknowledge and give it a name?
Pull up the string, and see it's a thing,
   yes, now you must give it a name.
Dig in your feet. Stare it straight down.
   Hold firm – it now has a name.
And whenever it tries to assume its disguise,
   let go, for you now know its name.

"I'm no good at math, my memory's lousy,
  my singing will not make you clap.
My fitness is bad, my spelling is sad,
  my sense of direction is crap."
We'll admit to most flaws, but some folks won't own
  the critical one in their pool.
There's rarely a day when you'll hear someone say,
  "Boy, I'm a gullible fool!"

The grandiose dreams of ten-year-olds
Involve fame, or space, or pots of gold.
But for me, my goal, when I had my way,
Was never to waste a summer's day.

Go to a movie, buy books you can read,
See halls filled with art, take a road where it leads.
A few dollars gets you enjoyment as true
As if years full of labor were all just for you.

Sometimes she found herself running straight from
  all those worries that kept her awake.
And sometimes she knew she'd be running straight to
  all those goals that she just had to make.
But linear living can't help but get old,
  so finally she let down her guard.
With nothing to lose, she kicked off her shoes
  and danced circles around in the yard.

You never know how long you'll stay
At lifetime's stops along the way.
So when you pause and take a knee,
Don't forget to plant a tree.

Bad habits often thwart prevention,
Even with the best intention.
Some you do for far too long,
Because you're not aware they're wrong.

In the name of 1, we must invoke 2,
   and 3 then, to even the score.
It's clear that the cause supersedes all our laws,
   it's preemptive, not paranoid, 4.
Down through the ages, the counting goes on,
   the way that it's always been done,
As the kings and the queens with their ends and their means
   forever start over at 1.

See me lost. See me found.
Pick me up and turn me 'round.
Point me younger through the maze,
And leave me lost in living days.

We can dream about soaring with birds on the wind –
   a lofty but futile goal.
But think of the things, which don't involve wings,
   that are fully within our control.
Like besting our nerves, and breaking the ice,
   and trying to make a crush real.
So with thanks to the birds, we muster the words
   to finally say how we feel.

Hike up a hill, and take any trail,
You'll end at the top, with never a fail.
But if you hike down, and take any way,
Where you'll end up – no one can say.

The children all giggle and duck back and forth
   as they peek around corners with glee.
But who is to say, this game that they play
   restricts the dimensions to three.
A quick look for us reveals things that are there,
   but they can see things that will be.
Such is the sound of kids peeking around
   the corners of time we can't see.

Missing the boat due to stark indecision
Governed his life with the utmost precision.
The major events in his past all had causes
That turned out to simply be ill-conceived pauses.

From paths that have crossed just a second too late,
    to your baby's first steps that you missed,
From shooting stars passed, to lightning too fast,
    to rainbows behind in the mist.
When there's only one chance, the solution is clear
    for not losing what wants to be found.
While the passing ships' plight can be blamed on the night,
    for us, we can just turn around.

Flake by flake, the blanket grows
    and shrouds each silent day.
It lingers still, and rests until
    it's time to put away.
We'll shake it out, and fold it up,
    and tuck it in a drawer.
And soon the spring will rise and bring
    the sounds of earth once more.

How can you tell whether something is true?
Start fresh with the facts and give logic its due.
Use a clean slate and keep bias at bay;
Pretend that you were in fact born yesterday.

One day she decided she'd write a new story,
   she built and developed a plot.
She added some twists and a character list,
   and decided what happened or not.
She relished the way she controlled all the moves
   and could choose between gladness and strife.
But though you might think there's a book filled with ink,
   she's just taking charge of her life.

They planted me gently the day you were born,
  together we've grown through the years.
When winds came on strong, you asked me what's wrong
  each fall when I shed all my tears.
And now we're both old, wrinkled, and worn,
  and leaning a bit to the side.
I hope that you know, I've enjoyed each day so,
  even though I have never replied.

Acknowledgements

Many thanks to: Jacob Barandes, Louis Deslauriers, Brian Hall, Theresa Morin Hall, Myra McLarey, Krissy Nimblett, Mala Radhakrishnan, Alexia Schulz, Corri Taylor, Rebecca Taylor, Jack Vance, Marina Werbeloff, and Carey Witkov. Also thanks to the Penguin Rhyming Dictionary by Rosalind Fergusson (1985), and RhymeZone www.rhymezone.com.